Kamloops

British Columbia's Riverside City

Chris Harris

text by Ken Favrholdt

Country Light Publishing
Discover British Columbia Books™

Designed, edited and typeset by Bill Horne

Printed and bound in China by Everbest Printing Co. Ltd.

Canadian Cataloguing in Publication Data

Harris, Chris, 1939-
 Kamloops

 (Discover British Columbia Books)
 ISBN 0-9685216-0-6 (bound)

 1. Kamloops (B.C.) – Pictorial works. I. Title. II. Series.

FC3849.K3H37 2000   971.1'72   C00-910476-3
F1089.5.K15H37 2000

Care has been taken to match this book's printed colours as closely as possible to the original 35 mm slides. The colours have not been digitally enhanced or altered.

OPPOSITE: *Kamloops' North Shore, with the Overlanders Bridge crossing the North Thompson River.*

OVERLEAF: *The Rocky Mountaineer arriving in Kamloops over the CNR Bridge.*

Contents

Acknowledgments

I would first like to thank Rebecca Lang who sparked the initial idea for this book. There are many others whose varied contributions I deeply appreciate. Special thanks to Dave Charlton of Rivershore Golf Course and Brian O'Keefe of Eagle Point Golf Resort, Elisabeth Duckworth of Kamloops Museum and Archives, Dave and Debbie Freeze, Kathy Humphreys and Bruce Dunn of the Kamloops Symphony Orchestra, Parks officer Ken Johansson, Nathalie Jones and David Low of Merlin Books, Don Larson of the Kamloops Blazers, Christopher Nicolson and Jamie Tattersfield of Sun Peaks Resort, Rob Purdy of the Kamloops Wildlife Park, David Ross of the Western Canada Theatre Company, Allan Stradeski, and Bruce Whyte of the Kamloops Cattle Drive.

The following models, friends and business people appear in the book or accompanied me on photo shoots, gave editorial help or made suggestions: Larry, Donna, Jeremy and Robin Brenner of JB Greenhouses; Ed Babcock, Sophie Babcock, Alexavria Darvin, and Linda Wrightson of Rainbow's Roost Organic Farms; Mike and Kay Carr, and Margie Child of Winter Green Farms; Melisa Caldwell, Darlene and Mike Calyniuk, Teresa Donk, Cole Fulmer, Rita Giesbrecht, Jacques Hull, Sheril Mathews, Ritti Prochnau, and Martyn Williams. I would also like to thank Claire Kujundzic and Bill Horne who put me up in their cozy home while Bill designed and edited this book.

The Secwepemc pit house models included Secwepemc Museum employee Dan Saul, Ben Belami, Jaimin Casmir, Kent Jules, Lillawas Jules, Eric King, Andrew Ned, Kellen Peters, Dailyn Swanson and Tyler Swanson. Darwin Atcheynum, Darcy Baker, Maggie Blackettle, Garon Dixon, Johnny Jackson and Kara John appear in the Kamloopa Pow-wow photographs. We were unfortunately unable to identify the dancer on page 40. If you know this young Pow-wow participant, please contact the publisher.

Very special thanks to Ken Favrholdt, manager and curator of Secwepemc Museum and Heritage Park and part time instructor of Geography at the University College of the Cariboo who wrote the text for this book and supported me throughout with creative suggestions and local knowledge.

Many thanks to Vic Hamm, president of the Kamloops Camera Club, as well as its members, for their ideas, support and participation in a photo contest for this book. Congratulations to Brock Nanson, competition winner, whose image appears on page 52. The black and white archival photos were reproduced courtesy of Kamloops Museum; catalogue numbers are attached for reference. Thanks also to Adam Stein, whose two winter Sun Peaks photos appear on pages 54 and 55.

Map data provided by Guy Doll and Ken Ward of KDW Geographic Solutions Ltd., official supplier of City of Kamloops Map Data, www.kdw.com. Map and panorama compositing by Bill Horne; slide scans by CustomColour, Vancouver, and Bill Horne.

The creation of the series "Discover British Columbia Books"™ has been greatly assisted by the corporate contributions of Lowepro. My sincere thanks to President Uwe Mummenhoff who supplied me with the most innovative and durable camera carrying equipment. Whether I travel by horse, raft, canoe, plane or foot, Lowepro continually makes the job easier.

ABOVE: *Downtown Kamloops reflected in the Thompson River.*
PREVIOUS LEAF: *August evening, Kamloops Lake.*

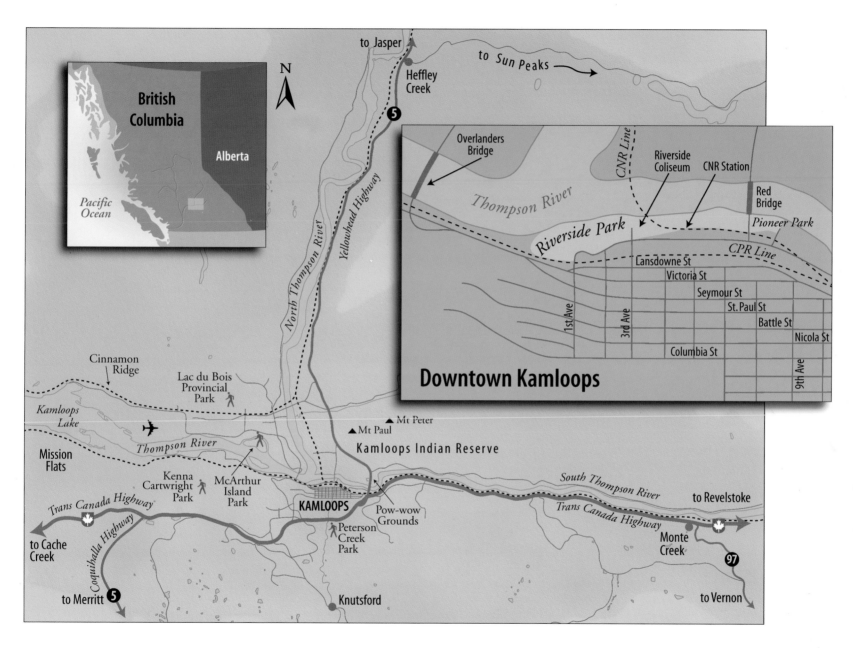

British Columbia

Alberta

Pacific Ocean

to Jasper

to Sun Peaks

Heffley Creek

5

North Thompson River

Yellowhead Highway

Overlanders Bridge

CNR Line

Riverside Coliseum

CNR Station

Red Bridge

Thompson River

Pioneer Park

Riverside Park

CPR Line

Lansdowne St

Victoria St

Seymour St

St. Paul St

Battle St

Nicola St

1st Ave

3rd Ave

9th Ave

Columbia St

Downtown Kamloops

Cinnamon Ridge

Lac du Bois Provincial Park

Kamloops Lake

▲ Mt Peter

▲ Mt Paul

Kamloops Indian Reserve

South Thompson River

to Revelstoke

Mission Flats

Thompson River

Kenna Cartwright Park

McArthur Island Park

KAMLOOPS

Pow-wow Grounds

Trans Canada Highway

Trans Canada Highway

Monte Creek

97

Coquihalla Highway

Peterson Creek Park

to Cache Creek

to Merritt **5**

Knutsford

to Vernon

Kamloops and area

Kamloops ~ past and present

Kamloops is an ancient place. Its name comes from the Secwepemc word "T'kumlups," referring to the confluence of the North and South Thompson rivers. The rivers have shaped the growth of both the Native and non-Native settlements, creating a natural site for the development of the sprawling urban centre that fills the valley today.

The early Secwepemc (or Shuswap people, as they have been more commonly known), were a semi-nomadic nation of 30 bands who lived along the rivers and lakes of BC's south-central interior. They relied on salmon, animals such as elk and deer, wild plant roots and all types of berries. Kamloops was one of their major centres.

Kamloops panorama, with Mounts Paul and Peter overlooking the city.

For thousands of years the valley was the home of the Secwepemc alone, who lived in riverine villages. It is not known how long people have occupied the valley although the earliest human remains date back 8,250 years. Prior to that, an ice sheet covered the landscape. If paleo-Indians lived in Kamloops before that time, they had likely moved south with the glacier's advance. Then, beginning about 10,000 years ago, the ice age waned and plants, animals and people reinhabited the landscape.

The first people of European ancestry arrived at Kamloops in 1811. They were fur traders, employed by the American-owned

ABOVE: *A group of railwaymen pose beside CPR Engine 96 at the Kamloops station.*

FACING PAGE: *Peterson Creek waterfall.*

Pacific Fur Company, which had its base at Astoria near the mouth of the Columbia River. Following a route up the Columbia and then by trail through the Okanagan Valley, they crossed the drainage divide to the South Thompson Valley, establishing a post at Kamloops in the fall of 1812. In the same year, the rival North West Company set up alongside the Astorians, and within two years eliminated its competition. The Hudson's Bay Company took over the North West Company in 1821. When HBC Chief Factor Samuel Black was killed in 1841, a decision was made to relocate the fort to the west side of the North River, as the North Thompson was then called.

In 1856, gold was discovered at Tranquille River. Within three years, large numbers of miners were coming through the Okanagan to Kamloops, followed by more newcomers via the Thompson Valley during the Cariboo Gold Rush. After failing to strike it rich, many disillusioned miners took up ranching and farming in the area.

In 1863 the Hudson's Bay Company moved its fort again. This time they set up on the south side of the river, just west of the present Overlanders Bridge named after the gold-seekers who passed through Kamloops the previous year. The Company hoped its new location would better serve the miners and settlers entering the area from the west and south.

During this period, paddle wheelers plied Kamloops Lake and the South Thompson River as far east as Spallumcheen. These boats, the first built in 1865 at Savona, reached their heyday during the construction of the Canadian Pacific Railway. The *Wanda Sue*, which now takes tourists along the Thompson River, is a modern version of these paddle wheelers.

When a transcontinental railway became the promise for BC's entry into Confederation in 1871, the CPR surveyed both the North and South Thompson valleys and along Kamloops Lake. In 1881 the railway chose its route through Kicking

1918

Main Street, 1912, now Victoria Street. Kamloops Centenary Parade celebrating the 100th anniversary of the first fir trading post.

Kamloops Indian Reserve, 1901. The "Passion Play" seen here consisted of a number of tableaux depicting the crucifixion of Christ. The Catholic Church organized this event which attracted hundreds of native people from different reserves in the Interior. The main village is seen here with St. Joseph's Church dominating the dusty street.

Conversation, Riverside Park.

16

Flower gardens in the heart of the city.

Horse Pass instead of Yellowhead Pass. This established the southside of the Thompson as the site of the future city.

Initially, settlers envisioned a townsite west of the Hudson's Bay Company fort at Mission Flats, so-named because of a Roman Catholic school built there in 1877. Across the Thompson River, pioneers James McIntosh and William Fortune built a water-powered mill to produce the much-needed commodities of flour and lumber. But it was east of the fort that Kamloops developed. McIntosh, realizing the CPR would have to pass through this area, foresaw the strategic location of the fledgling settlement and purchased 100 acres along the riverfront.

Other speculators formed a syndicate to purchase the large holdings of pioneer rancher John Peterson farther east, along the creek named after him. They proceeded to survey and subdivide the land in advance of the railway construction. The New Townsite Syndicate in turn sold part of the property to the railway in exchange for the CPR yards and station being located there. The new community quickly filled up and the station became the heart of town.

The Canadian Pacific Railway was finally completed through Kamloops in 1885, the mainline running directly

Waterfall, Peterson Creek Park.

down the middle of Main Street, now Victoria Street West. The construction of the CPR caused a wave of immigration and the town of 500 grew dramatically. Before long, McIntosh had built a town water supply, a telephone system was installed, and an electric light company formed.

The City of Kamloops was incorporated in 1893 with less than 1000 people, and the old and new town sites soon became one, growing slowly eastward where there was more land for expansion. The city bought James McIntosh's water-works in 1895 and took over the Electric Company the following year. By 1914 hydroelectric power was being generated at Barriere River to the north.

The old part of town, despite the construction of a new federal building along Main Street in 1901 (still standing), gradually declined. Lower property values made it feasible for the CPR to expropriate the river frontage, demolish older buildings, including much of Chinatown, and eventually in 1914 move its track to its present location.

In the boom years from 1900 through the Twenties, the City expanded south-ward and eastward. Post World War II prosperity led to the incorporation of the Village of North Kamloops in 1946.

Peterson Creek Park is within five minutes of downtown Kamloops.

Music at the Riverside Park bandshell.

Summer entertainment, Riverside Park.

Kamloops entered a new phase of its history in 1973 with the amalgamation of nine separate incorporated and unincorporated municipalities that now form the present city, making it the largest city in area in British Columbia at 296 square kilometres.

Since its founding Kamloops has had pretensions of becoming a major centre for the BC interior. It has sometimes had a reputation as a "cow-town", but in fact, it has long been an industrial town prospering on primary industries such as forestry and mining. The Kamloops Pulp Mill, for example, was built in 1964, and expanded in 1971 when Weyerhaeuser Canada purchased it. Afton copper mine on the west edge of the city was a major employer for twenty years.

Today, the service and education sectors are a major part of Kamloops' economy. Cariboo College was originally established in 1970 on the Indian Reserve, but within a year, moved to its current location overlooking the city. It achieved University-College status in 1989 and now grants degrees to a student population of over 5000 full-time and 2000 part-time students.

Kamloops continues to grow. The city's population is now well over 81,000, with approximately 1800 new residents arriving each year. Sustaining this many people is becoming a challenge. Although water is plentiful, concern for quality necessitates a new multi-million dollar treatment facility. In 1992 the city adopted WaterSmart, a water conservation program, and many Kamloopsians are discovering "xeriscaping" by using drought-resistant plants in their gardens. With good planning, respect for the city's heritage, and care for its environment, the future for Kamloops looks bright.

Summer evening, Riverside Park.

Summer in the city, Victoria Street.

ABOVE: *Towards Savona from Kamloops on the Trans-Canada Highway.*
FACING PAGE: *Leaving Kamloops at dawn.*

The Canadian Northern Pacific Railway, taking the Yellowhead Pass route through the Rockies, began construction through Kamloops in 1912. Its first passenger train passed through Kamloops Junction on the Indian Reserve November 24, 1915. After 1918, it became known as the Canadian National Railway. The CNR built a steel bridge and brick station in 1927 to serve downtown Kamloops, and today the bridge and station welcome the Rocky Mountaineer Railtours, seen above.

Kamloops is a major railway hub, with tons of freight from across Canada passing through its yards every year.

ABOVE: *Locomotives at work in downtown Kamloops.*

FACING PAGE: *The Third Avenue crossing over the CPR line.*

Weyerhaeuser pulp mill.

Wood chips destined for pulp.

ABOVE: *Shifting patterns, Weyerhaeuser settling ponds.*

FACING PAGE: *Mobile stacker with electrostatic precipitator at Lafarge Canada's Kamloops cement plant.*

The neighbourhood of Brocklehurst, with Lac du Bois Provincial Park behind.

The Kamloops Indian Band

The Kamloops Indian Band has always lived on the alluvial plain beneath Mounts Paul and Peter. Their villages of semi-underground winter homes ("c7i'stkten" in Secwepemcstin, also called kekulis or keekwillies in Chinook jargon) stretched along the South and North Thompson rivers. European and Canadian fur traders at Fort Kamloops numbered less than twenty for 50 years, compared to the 2000 Secwepemc. With the arrival of more settlers, the colonial government of British Columbia established the Kamloops Indian Reserve in 1862. It was not officially surveyed until a few years later, but the government did not recog-

nize the land claimed by the Kamloops Band, and in 1866 reduced their reserve to nine square miles. During the same period, a smallpox epidemic drastically reduced the Native population.

Christian missionaries, first the Jesuits in the 1840s, then the Oblates of Mary Immaculate in the 1860s, established missions to the Secwepemc. These Catholic orders attempted to create a model village with tight control over the tribe. By 1900 the Kamloops Indian Reserve had declined to a population of 600

PREVIOUS PAGE: *Children learn local First Nations history in a reconstructed pit house at Secwepemc Museum and Heritage Park.*

RIGHT: *Traditional dancing at Kamloopa Pow-wow.*

Kamloopa Pow-wow.

Kamloopa Pow-wow.

people, compared to the City of Kamloops with 3,000. In the nineteenth century the Kamloops Reserve was socially and economically isolated from the City across the River and the Band was restricted to life on the reserve. A bridge was finally built across the South Thompson River in 1887.

In 1890 the Catholic Church and the Canadian government established the Kamloops Industrial School. A major expansion took place in the 1920s when the present imposing brick buildings were built, and the name was changed to the Kamloops Indian Residential School. By the 1930s over 300 Native students were sent to the institution from various bands in the interior and elsewhere, making it one of the largest such schools in Canada. Like other similar schools designed to assimilate First Nations children, it is not without controversy.

Residents in the city across the river had little concern for the Indian Band. As early as 1907 some people were eyeing the relatively vacant land of the Reserve. The Board of Trade even proposed to take over the Reserve and move the Band elsewhere. Gradually the Band asserted itself and made plans for its own interests and development. Eventually, in the 1970s, the Department of Indian Affairs' role diminished, and the Band assumed more control.

In recent decades, economic progress has definitely come to the Kamloops Indian Band. The leasing of commercial property has become a large generator of revenue. The Band established its own industrial zone in 1963, the Mount Paul Industrial Park, with over 160 businesses. Sun Rivers Resort Community is a $600 million dollar master-planned development started in 1999 on the slopes of Mount Paul. It has a projected population of 5000, with a championship golf course.

The Band is also revitalizing its traditional culture. The former residential school, closed in 1978 and now called the Chief Louis Centre, is gradually being renovated for the Band's use and other First Nations organizations. The Secwepemc Museum is housed in part of the building. The huge log structure below the old school has been the site of the annual Kamloopa Pow-wow since 1993, a pan-tribal event attracting hundreds of performers and thousands of visitors to Kamloops. A Heritage Park on the site of a 2,000 year old village includes replicas of pre-contact Secwepemc winter homes, as well as unique ethnobotanical gardens.

In 1999 the Kamloops Indian Band purchased the historic Harper Ranch just east of the reserve, fulfilling the Band's claim since the 1860s. Since 1992, the Kamloops Indian Band and the City of Kamloops have abided by a Statement of Political Relationship, which is still being strengthened. The latest cooperative venture is the Rivers Trail, a project linking the City and the Reserve by a looped path along the rivers. Indian Point at the river junction will become a symbolic centre of the City and the Band — truly reflecting "T'kumlups".

Cherry Bluff reflection in Kamloops Lake.

Recreation and culture

Kamloops has always been a place where recreation and culture have delighted its residents and visitors. Everyone seems to play at something. Golf courses abound, sport fishing has been a traditional pastime for over a century, hockey is a perennial favourite, and mountain biking and snowboarding are increasingly popular. Skiing, both downhill and cross-country, is renowned. Live theatre and music are also growing, and regular arts festivals and exhibits continually take place.

ABOVE: *Fly fishing in one of the hundreds of lakes in the Kamloops area.*

FACING PAGE: *The 16th green at Eagle Point Golf Resort.*

The first team sport played in Kamloops was baseball, dating from the period of CPR construction. Horseracing became very popular in the 1880s at a racetrack on the Indian Reserve. The large British population favoured sports like cricket. The first polo match took place in 1890, also on the Reserve. Enthusiasts also formed clubs devoted to lacrosse, shooting, cycling, football, and tennis. Ice hockey was played on the frozen river as early as 1894.

Cycling routes and mountain bike trails are within easy reach of downtown Kamloops.

Summer at Sun Peaks Resort offers a variety of ways to experience its alpine meadows and scenery.

Sun Peaks village at night.

The first civic band was formed in 1885, followed by the Rocky Mountain Rangers militia who organized a marching band in 1903. There have been many other musical organizations over the years. An opera house built on Victoria Street in 1897 was the scene of many concerts, minstrel shows, plays and dances. Mohawk poet Pauline Johnson visited Kamloops and entertained in the Opera House in 1902; Hollywood star Boris Karloff of Frankenstein fame began his theatre career here in 1910.

Today, Kamloops is endowed with many fine facilities for sport and culture. Since 1985 Kamloops has promoted itself as the Tournament Capital of BC. Riverside Coliseum, opened in 1992, is the home of the Western Hockey League's Kamloops

Deep powder, Sun Peaks.

Riverside Coliseum.

Blazers, three-time winners of the Memorial Cup. The Aquatic Centre and Hillside Stadium are legacies of the Canada Summer Games held in 1993, Kamloops' Centennial year. They were followed by the Canadian Men's Curling Championship, the BC Games for Athletes with a Disability, and the BC Seniors Games, all in 1996, and the Men's and Women's World Curling Championships in 1997.

Kamloops has long been a city of many parks. It purchased land for Riverside Park in 1910, and a bathing pavilion was constructed in 1919 on the site of McIntosh's former Shuswap Milling Company. Mount Dufferin, now known as Kenna Cartwright Park, named after a popular mayor, is the largest municipal park in British Columbia. McArthur Island Park offers a variety of sport facilities and gardens. The Kamloops

Wildlife Park, a non-profit zoo dedicated to recreation, conservation and education, has over 70 species of wildlife, many indigenous to the area. Fishing brings many visitors to Kamloops in search of the *Kamloops trout* that have made the city famous. With two hundred lakes located within 80 kilometres, many with resorts and lodges, it is no surprise that the 1993 World Fly Fishing Championships were held here.

Sun Peaks Resort at Tod Mountain, located northeast of Kamloops, is an all-season mecca for a whole range of activities. With 900 vertical metres of skiing and an average of 559 cm of snow, it attracts alpine and cross-country skiers, telemarkers and snowboarders. Nancy Greene-Raine, Canada's female Athlete of the 20th Century, is the Director of Skiing.

The Kamloops Blazers face off against the Regina Pats in the Western Hockey League.

The Kamloops Symphony Orchestra in rehearsal at the Sagebrush Theatre.

In the summer, visitors to the European-style village can enjoy golf, tennis, and mountain biking, or events such as the Alpine Blossom Festival. Hiking is especially popular when the alpine meadows explode with flowers.

The Kamloops Symphony Orchestra has its headquarters at Sagebrush Theatre, and presents standard orchestral works, jazz, Broadway and seasonal favorites. The Western Canada Theatre Company has operated here for many years, as well as at the Pavilion Theatre, a second performance facility.

Kamloops at night.

Geology

People have long been attracted by Kamloops' landscape and geology. Native people observed and used minerals and metals long before the gold rush of 1858. The Secwepemc used ochre for making rock writings, or pictographs, and copper from a colourful bluff on Kamloops Lake for making bracelets and other decorative items. They also found gold at Tranquille River (now Creek). Bringing it to Fort Kamloops prompted the beginnings of a rush to the Interior. Long after the first prospectors gave up, Chinese miners reworked the gravel. During the Depression of the 1930s people still eked out a living along its banks.

The first important geological study of the area was made in 1871 by Dr. R.C. Selwyn, Director of the Geological Survey of Canada. By the 1890s, George Dawson, the next director of the Geological Survey, chose the region to create geologically

The white silt bluffs above the South Thompson River.

Kamloops Lake from Cinnamon Ridge.

accurate maps of the Kamloops and Shuswap areas that pioneered the use of colour.

The great outcrops of Mt. Paul and Mt. Peter are composed of mainly sedimentary rocks from the Triassic period. Before the close of the Paleozoic era 245 million years ago, the part of the

earth's crust which Kamloops sits on was located in the tropics north of the equator in the Pacific Ocean. It then moved to ancestral North America in the late Jurassic. We know this because of the presence of fossil crinoids, corals, and foraminifera that are found in a thick section of unmetamorphosed Devonian-Permian sedimentary and

Erosion patterns, Cinnamon Ridge.

volcanic rocks. Also, coral formations are found at the Lafarge Canada's limestone quarry east of the City.

Sugarloaf Hill, the prominent hump southwest of Kamloops, is part of a geological formation known as the Iron Mask Batholith, composed of gabbro, syenite and diorite. The 200 million year old intrusion is 20 kilometres long and roughly 4 kilometres wide. Its minerals, exposed at the surface, have attracted many mines to the area, from the early Iron Mask mine to the recent Afton, an open-pit copper-gold mine.

The rocks of Cherry and Battle Bluffs opposite each other on Kamloops Lake form an intrusive complex of a large volume of basaltic magma that is part of the Iron Mask Batholith. Other 60 million year old Tertiary rocks in the vicinity of Mara Hill and Tranquille caused Dawson to theorize about the existence of a volcano over what is now Kamloops Lake. In fact, about 52 million years ago, a basin was formed and occupied by an extensive lake. Subaerial volcanic activity built up materials filling the lake. Pillow lavas, volcanic bombs, plugs and dikes (this page) showing columnar jointing have intruded the sedimentary rocks along the south side of Mara Hill. Then, during the Miocene epoch about 15 million years ago, lava spread over much of the interior plateau from volcanoes in the Chilcotin region.

Dike, Cinnamon Ridge.

Fanciful shapes, Cinnamon Ridge.

During the Pleistocene epoch over the last two million years, an ice sheet covered the entire plateau, and was up to 1000 metres thick in places. When it retreated, the ice left a variety of deposits and lakes. In the Thompson River valleys one can see a series of terraces created after the last period of glaciation.

The "white silt" terraces (pages 60-61), as Dawson described them, consist of the sediments of a former lake bed that filled the Thompson valleys after the last ice age. This glaciolacustrine silt is up to 100 metres thick in the valley east of Kamloops. Here wind and water have sculpted extensive gullies, as well as hoodoos with their distinctive columns and cap rocks.

The horizontal lines on hillsides in the valley are known as terracettes, formed by a process of freeze-thaw and gravity, making the slope attain its natural angle of repose. Cattle are often seen grazing on these hills, making many people think animals are the cause.

Laughing rock, Cinnamon Ridge.

Hoodoo, Cinnamon Ridge.

Photographic interpretations, Cinnamon Ridge.

Architecture and heritage

Kamloops has a rich heritage which early historians recognized when they created the Kamloops Museum, one of the oldest in the province. But the rapid growth of the city in the 1970s and 1980s resulted in the loss of many older buildings, until the creation of a Heritage Committee. Now many buildings, including five that are City-owned, have been recognized for their heritage value.

The original Hudson's Bay Company fort has an interesting history. It used to be located on the Kamloops Indian Reserve, and part of it is now the area's oldest surviving building. For a while, the post-on-sill cabin functioned as the City's first museum, opening in Riverside Park in 1937, then moved when the present museum at Second Avenue and Seymour Street was built in 1957. The Kamloops Museum still exhibits the original log structure.

~~Father Le Jeune had St.~~ Joseph's Church built on the Kamloops Indian Reserve in 1900 on the site of the Jesuit Chapel established almost 60 years previously. The reserve village grew up near the church, and a cemetery dating from the 1840s lies to its south. Restored in 1985 by the Kamloops Indian Band, the ~~Catholic~~ Church is still in use and open to the public at selected times. ~~Father Le Jeune~~ resided in the rear of the church and published the *Wawa*, a quaint newspaper which carried stories from the reserves in the district and the Kamloops community.

The planting of trees, renovation of old buildings, and construction of new ones have helped revitalize downtown Kamloops. Many of the older structures still standing are made of local brick. Only a few century-old wooden buildings survive. St Andrew's Presbyterian Church (page 73), built on Seymour Street in 1887, was restored in 1998. In its heyday, the old Inland Cigar Factory (page 72), dating from 1895, employed twenty-five workers who produced 4,000 authentic Cuban-style cigars each day. The small brick building has seen many uses over the years, including a bakery, bookstore and bicycle shop. Diagonally across the street is the former Kamloops courthouse. Constructed in 1909, this grand brick and granite edifice with a slate roof is a designated heritage building, now operating as a hostel. The wood-panelled courtroom is open for the public to view. Contrary to popular belief, famous train robber Bill Miner was not tried in

St. Joseph's Church, Kamloops Indian Reserve.

The Old Cigar factory on First Avenue.

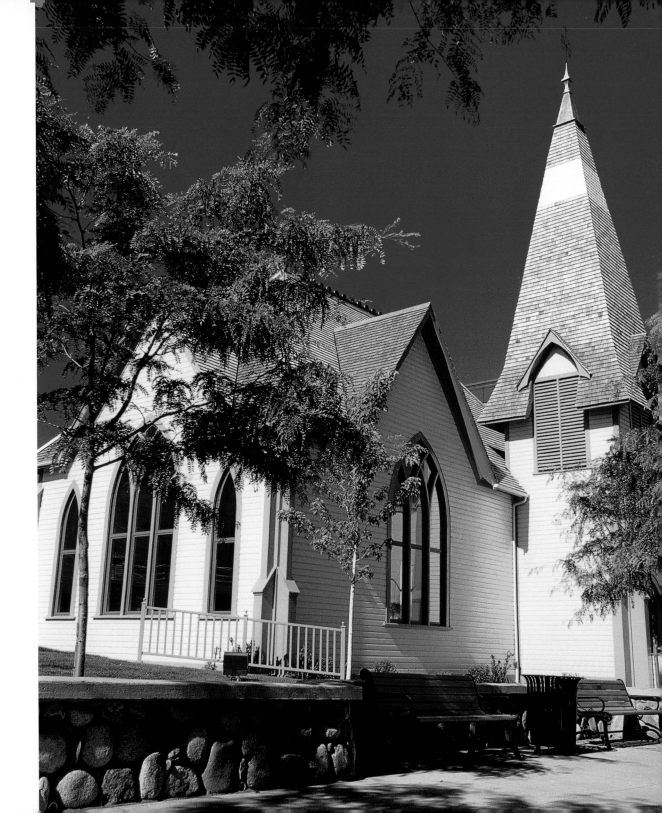

*St. Andrew's Presbyterian
Church, on Seymour Street.*

The Plaza Hotel built in 1927 remains a downtown landmark.

118 Victoria Street, originally the Imperial Bank of Commerce.

this building, but in an earlier courthouse where City Hall now stands. The original Bank of Commerce building (above), across from City Hall, was built in 1904. It later served as a police station and jail, City Hall from 1953 to 1964, then the City's Parks and Recreation office, until its conversion to a private business. Today it is a designated heritage site.

The Plaza Hotel (opposite), built in 1927 on the east side of downtown, was originally a tourist hotel in the Spanish mission style popular at the time, although the original roof was made of tin, not tile. In its glory days the rooftop lounge had wicker furniture and potted plants. The hotel declined in fortune over the years, but has now been restored as a "heritage hotel".

Considered a "skyscraper" when it was built, The Plaza is still one of the larger buildings downtown.

Beyond the city centre there are other areas with heritage sites such as the Chinese Cemetery which was once on the outskirts of town. Every spring, the local Chinese community holds the Ch'ing Ming festival to honour departed ancestors and give offerings of food, rice wine and paper money. Many Chinese died during construction of the Canadian Pacific Railway and in most cases their remains were sent back to their homeland. The location of the cemetery overlooking the Thompson River valley is felt to fit the ancient tradition of locating cemeteries according to the principles of Feng Shui and yin and yang.

ABOVE: *Knutsford Valley.*

FACING PAGE: *Storm over Knutsford.*

The Countryside

Kamloops lies in the heart of BC's "drybelt" where the region's semi-arid climate produces less than 25 cm of precipitation annually. Temperatures range from 37° C in the summer to -18 ° C in the winter. Ranching has traditionally been the main agricultural activity. Today there are approximately 150 ranches around Kamloops with an estimated 30,000 head of cattle. The livestock industry also includes sheep, dairy cows, hogs, fallow deer, bison and poultry. Exotic animals like llamas and ostriches have also been bred with some success.

Blackwell Dairy Farm is an example of a local industry that has created a niche for milk and other dairy products. But gone are the days of massive orchards for which Brocklehurst was famous until severe frosts destroyed the apple crop in the 1930s.

Old farm buildings in the hills near Kamloops.

Fence lines, Knutsford.

During the summer, a thriving twice-weekly Farmer's Market caters to customers who desire local, organic products. It has operated for over 20 years.

Kamloops has become known as the "ginseng capital" of Canada. Huge black cloths shade this crop and cover large areas that once grew alfalfa. Since 1982, when it was first planted, ginseng has become the region's second largest agricultural product, with 1000 hectares currently in production.

Farmers come from the surrounding area to sell local, ecologically - grown produce at the Kamloops Farmer's Market.

PRECEDING PAGE: *Mike Carr is one of several farmers who are reviving traditional methods such as ploughing with horses.*

OVERLEAF: *The grasslands of Lac du Bois Provincial Park.*

ABOVE: *Farmland, North Thompson valley.*

PRECEDING PAGE: *A Canadian National Railway freight train winds along the North Thompson river on its way from Kamloops.*

Dawn mist, North Thompson River.

Balancing Rock, near Savona.

A storm approaches Six Mile Ranch on Kamloops Lake.

Ponderosa pine, Kamloops Lake.

REFLECTIONS BY THE ARTIST

For some unknown reason, in the spring of 1999, instead of sending my books to Merlin's Bookstore through the mail, I drove to Kamloops to deliver them personally. While handing them over, I struck up a conversation with employee Rebecca Lang, who said to me, "why don't you do a photographic book on Kamloops? People ask for one almost every day."

Those words continually played on my mind as I drove home. As intrigued as I was, I had never photographed a city before, and as a wilderness photographer, I had plans to do a different book. One week later, however, I found myself returning to Kamloops to begin shooting. Where to begin, I asked myself? I started at the Information Centre, where I gathered maps and brochures. Then I went to Riverside Park and shot several rolls, including the image on page 16. All of a sudden, I was excited to be embarking on a new project.

Like many, I had only passed through Kamloops, never stopping to explore. Now I discovered a city surrounded by considerable areas of natural beauty. Nearby parklands such as Lac Du Bois, Kenna Cartwright, Riverside, and Peterson Creek, coupled with the city's many beautifully kept gardens, give one a feeling of being connected to the earth. This, together with its friendly native and non-native peoples, creates a most welcoming environment.

When I went to the Farmers Market, I immediately had a sense of what the surrounding countryside provides for Kamloops and what Kamloops provides for the rural areas. I realized that this is a city which offers the best of both rural and urban worlds. Residents can enjoy the recreational aspects of cycling, golfing, fishing and hiking, while on the same day attend a concert by the Kamloops Symphony Orchestra or a play at the Sagebrush Theatre. It wasn't hard to fall in love with Kamloops!

There were many highlights in my photographic explorations. I loved hiking through the fascinating geological formations of Cinnamon Ridge and the white silt bluffs, searching for artistic features of shape, colour, line and texture. I thoroughly enjoyed photographing farmer Mike Carr, who uses traditional methods to farm organically (page 80). His love for the land and the produce he and his wife Kay produce made shopping at the Farmers Market a more meaningful experience. The Kamloopa Pow Wow was the most powerful and significant event I have ever attended. I hope my images from that single day's shoot convey the deep respect with which these ancient traditions are celebrated.

From a photographer who used to merely pass through town, to a person who is now considering moving here, I say, thank you Kamloops.

*South Thompson River, from
the Yellowhead Bridge.*

COUNTRY LIGHT PUBLISHING

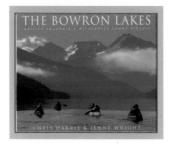

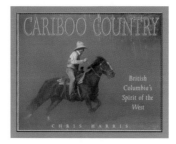

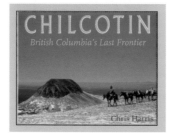

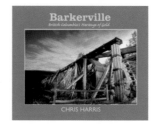

Discover British Columbia Books™

photography@chrisharris.com
www.chrisharris.com